AF207348

# *King's Last Visit* to Augusta

**He was persona non grata.**

**JOHN D. WATKINS**

**He was persona non grata.**

## JOHN D. WATKINS

MANHATTAN SOURCE PUBLISHING

*Augusta, Georgia*

Watkins, John D.,  Author
        King's Last Visit to Augusta / Written by John D. Watkins



Published in Augusta, Georgia, by Manhattan Source Publishing,
a division of Manhattan Source, Inc.
Augusta, Georgia

Cover illustration by Leigh Capps, Leigh Capps Illustrates and Designs,
Charlotte, North Carolina

**Library of Congress Cataloging-in Publication Data**

Watkins, John D. (John David), 1930-
        King's last visit to Augusta : he was persona non grata / John D. Watkins.
        p. cm.
Includes bibliographical references.

ISBN 1-891986-06-6 (alk. paper)
        1.  King, Martin Luther, Jr., 1929-1968. 2.  King, Martin Luther, Jr.,
1929-1968--Oratory. 3.  Campaign speeches--Georgia--Augusta. 4.  Poor People's Campaign.
5.  Augusta (Ga.)--Race relations. 6.  Augusta (Ga.)--Politics and government--20th century.
7.  Afro-American leadership--Georgia--Augusta--History--20th century.
8.  Watkins, John D. (John David), 1930-  I. Title.
 E185.97.K5 W325 2000
 323'.092--dc21

00-009409

Printed in the United States of America.

# CONTENTS

*John D. Watkins. Photo taken at about the time of the events of this book;
1968.*

# ACKNOWLEDGEMENTS

To my faithful and loyal secretary, Alberta Dunn Johnson, who has supported me in practically every endeavor undertaken during the past 30 years. The pictures of Dr. King and myself were taken by her on April 24, 1969 during Dr. King's appearance at Beulah Grove Baptist Church, Augusta, Georgia. My heartfelt thanks and appreciation.

I wish to thank other secretaries in my office, especially Kim Webb who deciphered the first manuscript of my thoughts as I remembered what happened thirty years ago.

I also wish to thank Dee Griffin, a news anchorwoman of WJFB, Channel 6, and Laurie Ott, anchorwoman of WRDW, Channel 12, both in Augusta, Georgia, for encouraging me to record my thoughts "before it is too late," of those fearful times when King last visited Augusta.

Paige Fleming, a Court Reporter for Brown's Reporting "fussed" at me constantly after she saw Dr. King's pictures, to write my thoughts about the meeting with Dr. King on March 24, 1968.

To Kathy Davis Watkins, who typed, retyped and retyped thoughts I had left out of the manuscript.

Thanks to Lester Strowbridge, business manager of Local 1137 and to Reverend B. I. Vernon, deceased, and to John Swint for bravely standing with me in defying those who opposed King's last visit to Augusta.

A special thanks to Blondell Condley and her mother, both deceased, whom I believe truly loved Dr. King, myself and the Southern Christian Leadership Conference (SCLC). They worked tirelessly to assure the success of our mission to bring Dr. King back to Augusta.

A very special thanks to my children, Crystal, David, Mike, Jack, Harriett, Brian and Leonard. During those turbulent years of the sixties, seventies, eighties and nineties, I tried to teach them who they are, from where they came, and how to prepare themselves for the future in America. I trust that I did the best that I could with them, and that they will, in some measure, come to appreciate what we tried to accomplish for their future in all our endeavors during the black revolution of the fifties and sixties.

# FOREWORD

I remember meeting John Watkins in Savannah, Georgia in the early fifties. He was an up-and-coming sophomore at Savannah State College, and very active in student affairs while he was Dean of Pledges and President of Alpha Phi Alpha Fraternity.

Savannah, Georgia, in the early fifties, was a hotbed for Civil Rights activities. I was a member of the local NAACP chapter and W. W. Law was its president. I remember distinctly meeting and discussing ideas with John at the NAACP meetings. W. W. Law was a dynamic leader–he inspired us to move against the deeply rooted oppression experienced by black people in every aspect of their daily lives. Segregation and Jim Crowism was everywhere and as repressive as ever. Black people were humiliated and degraded each and every day.

John and I both realized during that time that, even though the NAACP was effective, its actions were too slow for our burning desire to be free. We knew that a more direct approach was necessary if we were to witness meaningful change during our lifetimes. We went looking for someone who thought as we did.

We found that in Dr. King.

It was several years later that I reunited with John when he opted to support Dr. King and Southern Christian Leadership Conference (SCLC) in the early sixties. John was present when Dr. King spoke at Tabernacle Baptist Church the first time we journeyed to Augusta in

1962. John, Dr. King and I met and chatted in the church parsonage before the evening event. I was happy to learn that he had accepted my invitation to sponsor Dr. King in Augusta on March 24, 1968.

This book, though not as lengthy as most, is the product of a man who has "been there," "done that", and moved on to other things needing his attention. Although this book's primary purpose is to tell about Dr. King's last visit to Augusta, it is filled with accurate historical facts and it attempts to embrace the history of revolutionaries in America before and after America won its independence from England in 1776. Without much detail this book demonstrates the indomitable courage that men and women, black and white, displayed against overwhelming odds.

It is amazing to discover things in this book of which we were not aware previously. And to realize that we probably never thought enough about American history to truly ascertain who we are, how we got here, nor how we survived the hellishness of our times. The question now is, "Where do we go from here?"

It is my hope that every man, woman, and child in America read this book. That the schools will view it as a source of information about Dr. King that has never before been imparted to the general public. It will also be meaningful to those who think they understand Dr. King and the struggles he personally encountered. The story told in this book will add to their understanding.

Read this book and see if you can discover what Dr. King discussed with John on the evening of March 24, 1968 in an isolated motel in Augusta, Georgia. See if you can follow and understand the thoughts of these two men during that meeting. John's solemn promise not to reveal this conversation unless certain of Dr. King's ideas for the future were implemented still holds.

I commend you, John, for having the fortitude to tell it like it was. God bless you and all those who read your story.

Reverend Hosea Williams,
Atlanta, Georgia;  April, 1999

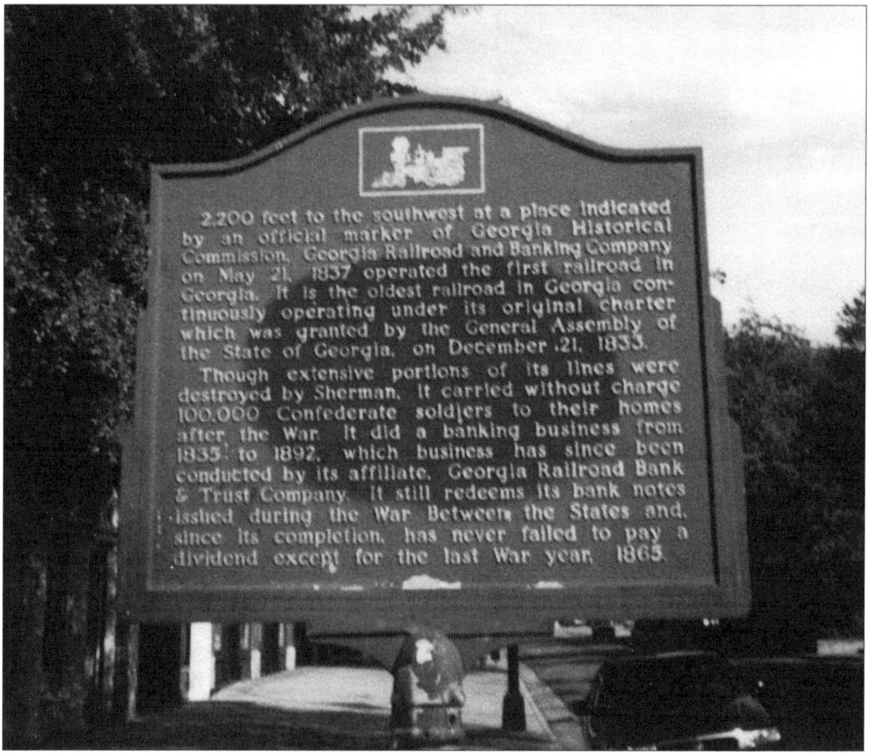

*First Union Bank building, formerly Georgia Railroad Bank & Trust.*

# PURPOSE

This book was written in an effort to enlighten those who really did not and do not understand the true meaning of the black revolution that occurred in America from 1954 until April 4, 1968.

It is the desire of this writer that this book appeal to and be read by the black masses in the hope that they will understand, and conceptualize the great character and mission of the person around whom that black revolution was centered, Dr. Martin Luther King, Jr. and the real purpose of the revolution. White people, when reading this book, will come to realize that we knew what the white leadership was thinking, how they, for selfish purposes, led other white people to believe our revolution to be about things that were so untrue.

It is also the desire of this writer that the black intelligentsia. will, in large numbers, understand the role they played in formulating some of the policies which directly or indirectly led to the assassination of Dr. Martin Luther King, Jr. The scurrilous and defaming attacks on Dr. King should have caused us to come to his defense. But in our quest to be *the first black this*, or *the first black that*, we unavoidably created a kind of schism among the leaders of the black revolution that turned the revolution into something it was not intended to be, and for the most part allowed our oppressors to ascribe to us motives which were utterly untrue. Even if our oppressors conjured up in their minds what they thought black people wanted, was it so great a difference from what they wanted that we would kill and murder the leader of the opposition to further our "real" motives? Of course not. Black people will never act in such a manner for such an isolated and decadent cause. The person of Dr. King and those who followed him were far above such barbaric thinking.

The purpose of the black revolution during the fifties and sixties was not to "mix" or "integrate" with white people. Its purpose was to desegregate America and achieve a sense of universal mobility without fear of mental or physical harm. It mattered not who would be where we had a right to go, or who owned the vehicle to transport us there. We wanted the equal opportunity to go wherever we might please, without having to face people who said we had no right to be there. We wanted the freedom to use whatever mode of transportation available, the freedom to choose.

If you were white, yellow, red, black or brown, and you were in a certain place, we wanted an equal right to be there simply because we knew it was a place to be. If you were there when we arrived, and you had a problem with us being there, fine. That was your problem, not ours. If you were not there when we arrived, that was also fine. But rest assured, our motives for being there were not because the opposition was there, but in spite of the fact that they were there. Americans journeyed to the moon at great expense for no other reason than that it was there.

The purpose of the black revolution was not clearly articulated by the leaders of the revolution. This fact allowed the opposition a great opportunity to portray a false and fearful impression of our motives, and most white Americans believed such portrayals to be true. They really thought our objective was to integrate with them–to be with them. How wrong they were! This propaganda gave a number of white people the impression that they were superior to people of color. They were wrong again, the Bell curve notwithstanding.

Our oppressors believed in their hearts that we wanted more than equality, but that we would settle for parity. And to this day a vast majority of white Americans think the same, and some blacks find this concept acceptable. We may have been gullible, but we are not stupid. It is now time that all Americans realize the real purpose of the black revolution, and the fact that many of us are willing to die as Dr. King did in pursuit of the realities of the revolution's original purpose.

To that end it is imperative that black American youth understand that in America, education is the most important tool he or she can achieve. To enable them to understand the real purpose of the revolution, they must be educated. The old saying that it is "who you know that gets you there, but what you know that keeps you there," is no longer appropriate, in vogue.

In order to survive in America independently of those who use us and to co-exist with them, it is imperative to get an education, no matter how or what sacrifices must be made. That goal should remain the top priority. Uneducated people have nothing to offer a civilized society, and will always be at the mercy of their oppressors. An uneducated person is easily misled, easily confused, easily frightened, easily dominated and subjected to the will of others. Uneducated people thrive on rumors, not facts. They will, most assuredly, lead a life of crime and imprisonment. They will be lazy without any constructive imagination, and useless to the human race of which they are a part. An uneducated people has no seriousness of purpose in life and therefore becomes a burden to the stronger of the species to which it belongs, eventually experiencing degradation, suffering and widespread destruction.

An uneducated people, having nothing of value to offer its own people or others, with no sense of purpose or direction, is usually washed ashore along with all other items given up by the "sea of life" as worthless creatures, unable to survive the mighty forces therein.

The purpose of the black revolution of the fifties and sixties was to free black Americans from the effects of the black codes and the "Jim Crow" laws enacted to prohibit black Americans from obtaining an education. These laws had the same result as slavery had had from 1619 until the Civil War.

Civilizations make progress by taking great leaps at specific times. We can harness the purpose of the black revolution by and only through education. If we will do so we will be prepared to take the great leap into the twenty-first century and perhaps challenge Bill Gates and others of that caliber, and take our rightful place amongst other great men and women of the human race.

# INTRODUCTION

*We hold these truths to be self-evident—that all men are created equal.*

*That they are endowed by their Creator with certain unalienable rights,*

*amongst these are, Life, Liberty and The Pursuit of Happiness.*

*–Declaration of Independence*

From its beginning in 1776, the United States of America has always had revolts led by patriotic Americans. They have been of various forms, for various reasons, led by people of various skin colors. Perhaps the greatest of all revolts was the American Revolution led by George Washington of Virginia. Supporters included John Adams of Massachusetts, Alexander Hamilton of New York, Benjamin Franklin of Pennsylvania, Thomas Jefferson of Virginia, James Madison of Virginia, James Monroe of Virginia, James Mason of Virginia and Patrick "Give me Liberty or Give me Death" Henry of Virginia, all of whose ancestors came from England and settled in America.

Their revolt against British rule, ushered in by the Declaration of Independence, brought independence to the Thirteen Colonies and all of the white people who inhabited those Colonies. It meant nothing to those inhabitants brought to America against their will and held in slavery within those Thirteen Colonies, nor to other persons of color. Not even for him who was the first to shed blood at the outset of the American Revolution, Crispus Attucks, a black Bostonian.

Because of their love for America, no slaves of African descent crossed over and joined the British during the Revolutionary War, despite the fact that they would receive their freedom if they were to join the British against the Thirteen Colonies. The slaves' love for America and America's promises during the American Revolution was apparently greater than their desire to be free. They would soon learn how shallow and meaningless those promises were, and that those who made them had no intention of fulfilling them unless they were forced to do so.

There are stories to the effect that over a thousand slaves owned by George Washington had decided to join the British during the American Revolution. But his distant cousin, Lund Washington, the manager of George Washington's plantation, persuaded them not to go with the "enemy." Lund Washington went aboard a British vessel to entertain and serve refreshments to the members of that British vessel in an attempt to prevent the crossover of the slaves. Lund was reprimanded by George Washington for meeting with the enemy, but Washington's slaves did not defect to the British. George Washington and his Revolutionaries, with the unshakable aid and support of France and the loyalty of black and white Americans alike, defeated England and rid the colonies of British rule. The colonies were freed from economic and political oppression.

The belief held by black slaves that the America they loved and helped to create was to be a land of freedom for all was shaken and almost obliterated when they learned that none of their kind were to be invited to the Constitutional Convention in Philadelphia in 1777-1787.

Black Americans were further bewildered when they learned that the Constitution, written by James Madison who would become the third president of the United States, and by James Mason, and adopted in Philadelphia in 1787, nowhere therein referred to them other than as certain laborers nor included them as equals with white Americans. The Constitution was not consistent with the Declaration of Independence, as Thomas Jefferson had written in the Declaration of Independence, when he said: "That all men are created equal and they are endowed by their Creator with certain unalienable rights, that among those are Life, Liberty and the Pursuit of Happiness." Those men (planters) at the Constitutional Convention lacked the moral courage to set us free.

In fact, that 1787 document specifically allowed trading in black human beings by white Americans and that "peculiar institution" known as slavery was allowed to continue for another twenty years, until 1808. It became obvious worldwide, and especially to thinking people in England and France, that the leaders of the Revolution, the authors of the Declaration of Independence, and those in attendance in Philadelphia who helped draft the United States Constitution in 1787 were all hypocrites, and that this document, adopted as the United States Constitution, was substantively deficient in that it sanctioned slavery. Unbelievable!

Thomas Jefferson, the Ambassador to France shortly after the Revolution, could not defend America's institution of slavery because he owned slaves himself. He rather gave the impression that he wanted it abolished. However, he knew it would not happen without great financial damage to himself. Therefore, he perpetuated it by continuing to own slaves, supporting the institution of slavery when he knew that it was immoral and wrong. Then, too, manumitting (freeing) his slaves would probably have been the end of his relationship with Sally

Hemings, a circumstance Jefferson could not accept. Come hell or high water, he would arrange for her to be with him in France.[1]

Black Americans at that time knew that if they were to be free and equal in America, it would come only if they personally led the fight to abolish the institution of slavery and its remnants.

The French Revolution and the revolt in Haiti sent a message to America that the same thing could take place in America if the institution of slavery continued. But as frightening as those revolts were to Americans, white Americans did absolutely nothing to demolish that "peculiar institution." Instead they tried to give religious sanction to this evil. (Men never do evil so thoroughly and completely as when they do it from a religious conviction.)

Picture, for a moment, the pain and suffering black Americans undeservedly encountered during those terrible times, and they survived physically. We are still wrestling with the damage slavery did to the minds of black Americans. We cannot understand nor accept how our ancestors became slaves in the first place. Some of us cannot discuss it without anger and contempt. But we must be able to discuss it in order to prepare ourselves and our children for the future in these United States.

---

[1] The delegates at the Constitutional Convention in Philadelphia in August of 1787 compromised on slavery and wrote i n the Constitution that the slave trade was to continue for twenty more years; that slaves (us) would be counted as 3/5 of the total population. All of us together was only worth 3/5 of the white population for representation in the House of Representatives.

It would be almost another hundred years before the next great revolt would occur in America so that the badge of slavery could be physically eliminated from within the United States. It took revolutionaries like Dred Scott, Nat Turner, "preacher" and forerunner of the Civil War, Gabriel Prosser, Harriet Tubman, Sojourner Truth, Denmark Vesey, Harriet B. Stowe, Horace Greeley, William L. Garrison, Frederick Douglas, John Brown, and most of all, Abraham Lincoln, with the help of  other northern abolitionists, to assail and destroy this pernicious institution. And in doing so, 620,000 Americans gave their last "full measure of  devotion."

There were 360,000 lives lost by the Union in the destruction of slavery, and 258,000 lives lost by the Confederacy in its defense of slavery. More than 50,000 civilians in the South were killed. Some 40,000 black soldiers gave their lives as they fought for their freedom on the side of the Union. This caused the Confederates to dislike, despise, and even hate black people. Many blamed the black people for the fact that they fought, died and suffered defeat in the Civil War.

There is no evidence that black Americans fought and died in the defense of the Confederacy. Under Jefferson Davis, the Confederacy finally and reluctantly decided to enlist the black slave to fight for the Confederacy in late March 1865 in exchange for freedom. It was too late. Grant and his army of white and black soldiers were gaining on Richmond because the fall of Petersburg had just occurred.

A memorial dedicated to those black Americans who fought and died for the Union during the War of the Rebellion (Civil War, 1861-1865) was dedicated in July, 1998 in Washington, D.C.  In attendance for those services was this writer, and Lee Hannah, and Orienthal A. Hannah, sons of Mrs. Kathy Davis Watkins, of Louisville, Georgia.

There stills stands an auction block in Louisville, Georgia, the first capitol of Georgia, where slave trading was a daily routine before the War of the Rebellion (Civil War). (Go see it and take your children.)

From 1865 to 1877 (the Reconstruction period) it was incorrectly thought that there was no further need for revolutionaries in America, especially black revolutionaries. The consensus was that since slavery had been abolished and the Freedmen Bureau created, black Americans would take their rightful place in the socio-economic and political life of America. It never happened! Instead thousands of blacks were killed by the remnants of the Confederacy.

Without the assistance of the United States government during Reconstruction, (1865-1877) the Freedmen recognized that they needed black pioneers. Little did the Freedmen know, or wanted to believe, that their government would one day abandon them and allow those who once held them in slavery, who fought and died by the hundreds of thousands to keep them there, once again to control their destinies.

President Andrew Johnson, President Ulysses S. Grant and President Rutherford B. Haynes, during the period of time from 1865 to 1877, either agreed, acquiesced or participated in the restoration of power to the same old racist bigots who had oppressed blacks for 250 years. During this period the duly-elected black and white representatives in the legislatures of the rebellious southern states were ousted through violence and intimidation, a practice that has continued to some extent in many southern states even until today. These same rascals, using similar methods of violence and intimidation, brought to an end our black representatives in the U.S. Congress, and, for decades thereafter, there were no blacks in the U. S. Congress to represent black Americans. And blacks elected to state legislatures in the Confederate

States were ousted by white men who had guns. Blacks had no guns at that time.

It is estimated that over twenty thousand black men, women and children were murdered in the Confederate states by white men between 1868 and 1877.

This deplorable situation would have been much worse had it not been for black women…wives, mothers, lovers, and sisters… and a few dedicated white women opposed to the sordid treatment black Americans faced in their daily lives. They used their positions, their strength, talent and finances to teach, train and educate four million liberated black men, women and children. They enabled the black populace to survive such violent and painful times. It was, as Fredrick Douglas stated, a time of "Root little pig, or die." And died we did. Our people had no way to defend themselves. The Federal government abandoned us and we were left to the mercy of the immoral white men who persecuted us without mercy.

Black pioneers who sprang up during the following fifty or sixty years, such as Paul Roberson, Marion Anderson, Booker T. Washington, W. E. B. Dubois, Mary McCloud Bethume, Benjamin Mays, Mordecai Johnson, Walter White, Adam Clayton Powell, James M. Hinton, Sr., Ralph McGill and countless others, had minimal effect on racial bigotry. Black Americans were still being lynched, raped, kidnapped, whipped, tarred and unjustly jailed by the southern white men. They were the last to be hired, and the first to be fired. And in many instances, when blacks did work, they were cheated out of their wages by southern whites. And the federal government did nothing!

During the Truman, Eisenhower and Kennedy administrations, black people of America recruited black revolutionaries to attack the institution of racism and Jim Crowism, the obvious remnants of the slave system. Some of these revolutionaries were Gunner Myrdal, Thurgood Marshall, Charlie Houston, Waitres Warring, Donald Hollowell, Constance Baker-Motley, Elijah Mohammed, Malcolm X, Stokely Carmichael, C. S. Hamilton, James Farmer, H. "Rap" Brown, Ralph D. Abernathy, Whitney Young, Julian Bond, Jesse Jackson, Cleveland Stokes, Gary Hatcher, Angela Davis, Charles Diggs, and Dr. Martin Luther King, Jr. There were many others, far too many to mention in this short treatise.

This book depicts an episode in the life of Dr. Martin Luther King, Jr., shortly before his assassination, and this writer's involvement in that particular episode. It is being told thirty years after King's death. It is told now because it has been too painful for this writer to actualize and write about the reality of King's last visit to Augusta. His one-on-one conversation with this writer during the evening of March 24, 1968, was so impressive that it is hard for me to fathom that ten days later he would be dead.

All of the heartaches and agony I experienced in bringing Dr. King to Augusta are deeply rooted in the recesses of my mind and require almost an implosion of my soul to recall them. Doing so creates emotions that are indescribable.

I have desired to *not* cause any distress to the families of those persons who could have, but did not, assist in this great effort. These persons have all gone now, and I feel extremely comfortable in finally writing this story as so many have urged me to do.

*The Confederate Memorial stands in the middle of Broad Street, Augusta, GA.*



*The Augusta
Chronicle
News Building*

# ONE
## POLITICS IN AND AROUND AUGUSTA IN 1968

*Four score and seven years ago, our Fathers brought forth upon*

*this continent a new nation, conceived in Liberty and dedicated*

*to the proposition that all men are created equal.*

*–Lincoln's Gettysburg Address*

Augusta, Georgia and surrounding Columbia County, Georgia; Aiken County, South Carolina; and Edgefield County, South Carolina in 1968 were places of intense development of the Republican Party. A continuation of that party and its philosophy as set forth under U.S. Senator Barry Goldwater, who was the Republican Party's candidate for president of the United States in 1964, had engulfed Augusta, Georgia to the great satisfaction of the influential Augusta Chronicle and its publisher, William Morris, and editor, E. Harris.

Goldwater ran against Lyndon B. Johnson who was then President as a result of the assassination of President John F. Kennedy in November, 1963. Johnson had been Kennedy's vice president. It is this writer's opinion that the philosophy of the Republican party was then (1968), and is now, almost identical to the philosophy of the Democratic Party in existence just before, during, and after the Civil War (the War of Rebellion, 1850-1865): ***Keep the black man in his place.***

The assertive philosophy of the Democratic Party at that time (1832-1865) was a states' right of nullification of any Federal law which touched on slavery with which the southern states disagreed; and the states' right of self-determination without interference from the Federal Government. This was a cover. Its main purpose was to retain and perpetuate slavery in defiance of any Federal law which was anti-slavery. The southern states were determined to continue to engage in the slave trade and to force the Federal government to enforce the 1850 Fugitive Slave Act; that is, the Federal government would assist in the return of runaway slaves to the plantation owners, no matter the reason they fled, or in what state or territory they might be found. The State of Georgia vowed during that time, that "upon the faithful execution of the Fugitive Slave Act (by the Federal Government) depends the preservation of our  beloved union."

This law (The  Fugitive Slave Act), more than anything else, caused Harriett Beecher Stowe, a white woman who was fed up with the institution of slavery, to write "Uncle Tom's Cabin." That book was widely read and gained her an audience with Abraham Lincoln, who, upon meeting her exclaimed: "So you  are the little lady who wrote the book that started this great war." But then that is another story to be told at another time and another place by this writer or someone else who depreciates having his ancestors subjected to being owned by another human (inhuman) being. That too, is another story, or series of stories that  were going on from 1619 to 1865. Let us return to 1968.

In 1968, the sprawling Savannah River Plant in Aiken County, South Carolina, just across the Savannah River from Augusta, Georgia, employed some 15 to 20 thousand scientists, engineers, mathematicians, laborers, and skilled workers who teamed together to make tritium and plutonium, ingredients for the atomic bomb. These people were, for the most part, Republicans.

The entire area was the home base of Strom Thurmond from Edgefield, South Carolina, the segregationist Senator who had bolted the Democratic Party in 1948 because of his dislike for the Civil Rights plank in the Democratic Platform. For that reason he ran against Truman as a candidate for the Dixiecrats. In his acceptance speech in Alabama in 1948 as a Dixiecrat candidate, Thurmond proclaimed that white people in the south would never accept black people into their homes, schools and swimming pools. Oh! How he misunderstood us!

The former Democrat then ran for U. S. Senator from South Carolina as a write-in candidate in 1954, and won because of his unyielding stand for segregation. He was then, and is now, a staunch segregationist. (A leopard never changes his spots–he camouflages them very well as Thurmond has done during the past ten or more years in order to obtain black votes in South Carolina.) He had been winning before by the vote of South Carolina white citizens. Blacks in South Carolina, in the forties and fifties, were not allowed to vote freely. They can vote now but will they vote to replace Thurmond as they should do?

During the presidential election of 1964, Senator Thurmond helped to revolutionize this area and change it from a Democratic stronghold to a stronghold of the Republican Party. His efforts enabled

Goldwater to defeat Lyndon Johnson in this part of the country with a strong showing in 1964, even though Johnson won the presidency by a landslide.

Of course, President Eisenhower's visit to the world-renowned Augusta National Golf Course, the establishment of a Mamie Eisenhower cottage on the grounds of the Augusta National, and the Augusta National's racist policies, played an important role in transforming this area into a favorable place for the National Republican Party during the late fifties and early sixties. Ronald Reagan was also a frequent visitor while he was president, but discontinued his visits after a man crashed a gate at the Augusta National in order to gain an audience with him.

The conservative (racist) policies of those who called themselves Republicans (doing away with welfare and embracing the code words "law and order") during those years were the same policies of the present day Republicans (against affirmative action, set-asides, and affirming further attacks on welfare).

The Augusta National Golf Course, home of the prestigious Master's® Golf Tournament, founded by legendary golfer Bobby Jones, was, and is to this date, a bedrock of racism and sexism. For many years it had no black members and no women members. "We don't want any g… white women coming up here telling us what to do," one member relayed to this writer, as the reason there are no women. He gave no reason why there were no black members, for he and I both knew, without saying it, why there were no black members for so long. The Augusta National finally accepted a black person as a member. Vernon Jordan is a frequent guest of various members and played golf there during the past ten (10) years.

Across the South, in local elections, white democratic candidates prevailed because of the swing vote of the die hard black democrats and their black supporters, even though they received absolutely nothing from the white democratic candidates they helped to get elected. The black leaders, of course, had been paid off by the white political bosses for delivering to the "Boss's" candidates the black "Bloc" vote. This has been particularly true in the city of Augusta, Georgia.

Blacks, in 1968, for the first time in history, held one or two elected offices in Augusta,Georgia, but none in Aiken County,  or Edgefield County, South Carolina, nor in Columbia County, Georgia, even though they make up more than 50% of the population in some of those counties that surround Augusta.  Columbia County, Georgia still has no black elected official—what a shame! This situation continues to exist throughout the south… clearly amounting to taxation without representation, the spark that ignited The American Revolution.

Augusta, located on the Savannah River, is the easternmost major city in Georgia other than Savannah and Brunswick. It is across the river from the infamous former town of Hamburg, South Carolina, a place where Freedman were massacred during Reconstruction by white mobs from Edgefield and Augusta to prevent the creation of a town of blacks to be run by blacks.

Augusta is also the city which General Sherman, during the War of The Rebellion (Civil War) wanted everyone to believe his army would attack during the fall of 1864 when he left burning Atlanta, on his famous "March to the Sea." General Sherman's left flank, under the command of General Slocum, only feigned coming to Augusta, confusing Confederate General Braxton Bragg (Ft. Bragg, North Carolina is named for him.) Bragg had been assigned to defend Augusta where a confederate arsenal was located. It is rumored that the reason Sherman did not bring his army to Augusta was because he had a girlfriend here. Sherman later denied this rumor and stated it was purely a military decision not to bring his army to Augusta. But he could, so he stated, if Augustans desired it, reassemble his army and travel to Augusta. He never received a reply to this suggestion.

Augusta was also the home of segregationist Roy Harris, an attorney and one time Speaker of the House of the Georgia General Assembly. Harris also published a newspaper in Augusta named *The Augusta Courier*. In it he blatantly published white supremacist views and ugly cartoons of important blacks who were seeking changes in this anti-Black area. The purpose of these cartoons was to "poke fun" at black Americans and diminish their importance in the eyes of white people and to make white people less friendly and too ashamed to be with or around black Americans. It worked and is working in America to this day. Not wanting to be with us or around us is their problem, not ours, "for we are here to stay."

*The Augusta Courier* portrayed black Americans in cartoons including caricatures of how blacks would appear as a state trooper gave a speeding ticket to a white woman. Harris, with the help of other prominent whites, organized the White Citizen Council in Mississippi in 1954. The aim of the White Citizen Council was to stop the desegregation of public schools and oppose, in any manner, the enforcement of the public accommodations laws throughout the South.

Roy Harris, a cigar smoker, strong supporter of Herman Talmadge, one-time governor of Georgia, was a small indomitable rotund figure. He once debated Julian Bond. Harris was political "King Pen" in Georgia during the existence of the county unit system, and he prophesied that integration of the races would bring about mongrelization. White people in Georgia accepted this theory and relentlessly fought the 1954 school desegregation decision for more than two decades. Charlyne Hunter and Hamilton Holmes (now deceased), with the legal push of the NAACP and Donald L. Hollowell, a prominent Civil Rights attorney, entered the University of Georgia to the dismay of Harris and his followers.

A picture or portrait of Roy Harris was on display in the United States District Court House in Augusta, Georgia for many years. Harris was also the senior partner in a law firm in Augusta, out of which came a local Superior Court Judge who presently sits on the bench of the Augusta Judicial Circuit. It is unlikely that this judge's attitude would be different from that of Roy Harris. In fact, he often displays the same kind of attitude while sitting on the bench in judgment of black Americans. From the bench he often refers to the leaders of the Confederacy, and particularly to the Generals of the Army of the Confederacy. His last name is the same as that of the Confederate General who led the infamous charge of Gettysburg.

Augusta, Georgia is also the home of George Walton and Button Gwinnett, two of the signers of the Declaration of Independence. It is also known as a city in love with the Confederacy and its cause. This love is symbolized by the erection of a 60-70 feet tall marble memorial in the heart of the city of Augusta on Broad Street, atop of which are lifelike statues of Confederate Generals Robert E. Lee, Stonewall Jackson, A. P. Hill and A. H. Johnson. A bridge across the Savannah River that connects South Carolina with Augusta is named after Jefferson Davis, the president of the confederacy.

Across Broad Street from The Confederate memorial is the News Building, home of *The Augusta Chronicle*, known during the Civil War as the *Augusta Constitutionalist.* Less than a block up Broad Street from this monument is one of the oldest banks in Georgia. The Georgia Railroad Bank & Trust Company, now known as First Union. This bank assisted in financing the Confederacy during the Civil War.

There is a historical marker on Broad Street to the south of the Confederate memorial calling attention to slaves during Thackery's visit to Augusta in 1856, and thereon are these words: "In the 'Masonic Hall' on this site, the British author lectured (Feb. 11-12, 1856) as guest of the Young Men's Library Association. He wrote home: 'Nice quaint old town, Augusta, rambling great street 2 miles long, doctors and shopkeepers the society of the place, the latter far more independent and gentleman like than our folks, much pleasanter to be with than the daring go ahead northern people. Slavery, nowhere repulsive, the black faces invariably happy and plump, the white eager and hard. I brought away 60 Guineas for 2 hours talking, a snug little purse from snug little Augusta."

No man or women is happy being the slave of another. This was propaganda orchestrated by Augustans to impress Thackery.

There is a concrete pillar on the corner of Broad and 5th streets that is called the "whipping post." It supposedly got its names because black slaves were tied to this post and whipped publicly. Can you imagine such a spectacle?

Dr. King had visited Augusta two or three times before March of 1968. The first time he came, he spoke at the famed Tabernacle Baptist Church on Gwinnett Street (now Laney-Walker Boulevard). People came from every county, city, town, and hamlet in the Central Savannah River Area to hear him.

During his first visit to Augusta in 1962 there were approximately 10,000 to 12,000 people trying to get into the church to see and hear him. People occupied all the pews in the church, downstairs and the balcony. They lined the walls and the halls, and the basement was bursting with people. Such a mass of black people and cars outside the church had never been witnessed before that time in Augusta, nor since except for King's last visit to Augusta in March of 1968.

In March of 1968, Dr. King believed that because of Augusta's black leadership's feeling toward him, he was not welcome to return to Augusta. The black leadership felt that King's outspoken stand against the Vietnam War which they never understood, and his proposed Poor People's March on Washington, would somehow alienate them from, and damage their relationship with Augusta's white power structure. This white power structure was  anti-King in every aspect. King apparently concluded that further visits to Augusta would not be fruitful and that Augusta, because of the black leadership's dislike of him, was outside of his sphere of influence.

However, Augusta was somewhat like Chicago: the black clergy there shunned King. But he was willing and eager to visit Augusta again in an attempt to get Augusta's black population on the bandwagon in support of the Poor People's Campaign on Washington which was rapidly approaching.

*The Thackeray Plaque*

*The Haunted Pillar;*
*"the whipping post."*

*The Haunted Pillar of the Lower Market*

# TWO
## THE CALL AND
## THE ACCEPTANCE

*Men should not be judged by the color of their skin,*

*but by the content of their character.*

–Dr. Martin Luther King, Jr.

At approximately 5:30 a.m. on the morning of March 20, 1968, the telephone in my bedroom rang several times. Finally I picked up the receiver, and said, "Hello."

"Hello," the caller said. "Is this John… John Watkins?"

I said, "Yes, this is he. To whom am I talking this early in the morning?"

"This is Reuben, Reuben Gamble. Do you remember me… Gamble from Vidalia."

I asked, "Reuben… Vidalia… John Byrd's homie… Savannah State College… Jewell Gamble's brother?"

Well, who could forget the beautiful Jewell Gamble, I thought, or the eccentric John Byrd who were in attendance at Savannah State College when I was there.

"Yeah! Yeah! Sure, now I remember you, Reuben, long time no see you, your sister or John Byrd," I said, finally waking up.

"What did I do to deserve this wake-up call?" I asked.

"First let me apologize for calling this time of morning–but it is important," he said apologetically. "Hosea Williams called me last night and said Dr. King wanted me to ask you to sponsor him at a rally in Augusta, Saturday, March 24th–to raise money for the Poor People's Campaign. I am on that committee. You do know about the campaign?" Reuben asked in that rapid stuttering voice of his.

Surprised and flattered–I sat up in bed, now wide awake.

"Sure I know about the Poor People's March on Washington, but it has not been publicized in Augusta," I said.

"That is why Dr. King wants to visit Augusta–to get support for the march," Reuben stated. "And he wanted to know if you would take on the responsibility of sponsoring him there this coming Saturday," he asked.

I was still in a state of shock.

"Today is March 20; that is such short notice. Why didn't they contact me earlier?" I asked.

"I don't know, but we certainly need your help now. The campaign is not going too well at this point. There is a deliberate effort by some to stop the Poor People's March on  Washington," he said.

"I know. You hear all kind of things but you certainly cannot allow rumors about Dr. King to destroy such a noble effort, or for that matter, dampen our spirits about achieving equality in America. We have come too far, for too long, to stop and give up now. That is not King's personality and most assuredly, it is not mine," I said, as I now sat up on the side of my bed.

I was well aware of a small effort in Augusta by a few persons, mostly women, to support the Poor People's Campaign. But not one black male leader here had voiced support for Dr. King and the Poor People's March on Washington, even though the news about it had spread throughout Augusta.

"Won't you help us out?" Reuben pleaded. "I know the time is short and we apologize for that but he wants to come to Augusta, and you are our only hope," he continued.

"I don't know what I can do since time is so short, but let me make some contacts to ascertain which church or auditorium would be available on Saturday after I get to the office, and I will call you back sometime before five. I cannot make any promises, Reuben, the black leadership here is opposed to Dr. King."

"Do this for Dr. King, John," Reuben said in a voice with a slight hint of condescension.

"I want to, Reuben, but it will be difficult to get support for Dr. King or cooperation from those who can help him here in Augusta. I'll give it my best shot," I said.

"Thanks, John. I will call Hosea and ask him to put Augusta on the schedule for this coming Saturday. Could you shoot for 2:30-3:30?" he asked.

"I will try, Reuben. You know this will seem like we are imposing. So what if it does," I said. "He needs to come back to Augusta, it would help a lot. I will call you back. Take care."

"I'll be waiting for your call," he said. And then we both hung up.

I sat there thinking about King, Rosa Parks, Reverend Shuttlesworth, the many lives lost, the Montgomery bus boycott, the sit ins, the demonstration, by Paine College students, Didley getting shot as we demonstrated at H. L. Green on Broad Street, the Selma March, and how we were indebted to King who had been stabbed and jailed many times, along with many others. I thought about the SCLC, and the 1964 Civil Rights Act, the act that allowed blacks to enter and be served at all restaurants catering to the general public, and all other public accommodations. And now he was being rejected by those who benefited  from the passage of that bill which was enacted by Congress and signed into law by Lyndon Johnson–all as a direct result of King's leadership.

I could see Bill Conner and the dogs attacking men, women and children as they marched with King for Freedom in Birmingham, Alabama. How King had been charged, tried and acquitted of Alabama tax law violations. "Now is the time for all men who believed in our revolution to come to the aid of Martin Luther King, Jr.," I thought.

Finding a place for King to speak posed a dilemma for me because I knew that the largest black churches in Augusta, Tabernacle Baptist Church, Thankful Baptist Church and Springfield Baptist Church, all churches that could accommodate large crowds, would not welcome him. Two of the three  pastors of those churches were involved with the white political power structure and would not allow him to come to their churches out of fear that his presence would damage their relationship with the "white powers that be." The pastor of Springfield Baptist was not involved in that way, but his church might not be the best choice for this meeting.

Further, Paine College was another option, but being a predominantly black college with a white President, Clayton Calhoun, who thought King's views were extreme, it was doubtful if Dr. King would be allowed to speak there. The president would probably be afraid that students would demonstrate against him and request his removal as president of Paine. "But," I thought, "I must ask."

*Tabernacle Baptist Church*

*Thankful Baptist Church*

*Paine College (as it is today).*

Springfield Baptist Church

# THREE
## Preparations For The Visit



*Ask not what your country can do for you,*

*but ask what you can do for your country.*

*–John F. Kennedy*

I thought long and hard about this situation on the way to the office; about the names of those who could assist me. The names of men and women who would gladly participate, but had very little influence in those churches, came to mind–John Swint, a small department store owner; Lester Strowbridge, a union business representative; B. Bryant and Charlie Reid, black businessmen who pledged their support; Topsy Eubanks, a civil rights activist; Reverend B. L. Vernon, a black minister, pastor of the Beulah Grove Baptist Church; Blondell Condley and her mother; as well as the mother of King Rowe, a popular radio announcer, came to mind.

When I arrived at my office I had decided how I would make contact with the pastors of those three churches without confronting them directly. So, I asked one of the secretaries in my office to get the names and telephone numbers of the chairman of the deacon boards of those churches. I would contact each one of them, and if I could persuade them to assist, they in turn would exert their influence on their pastors.

Lo and behold! I quickly discovered that these people were also involved in a Black Voter's League, whose purpose was to get Blacks registered to vote and then get them to the polls on election day to vote for their Boss's choice. The largest of those black voters leagues was controlled by a white political boss by the name of John Murray who was called the "cookie man", because he owned Murray Biscuit Company in Augusta and employed 100 to 150 blacks, if not more. Many of those employees were members of this "Citizen Voters League" as it was called.

Contact was made with one after another, but our requests were denied. I felt ashamed to be from Augusta at that time. I became angry at the pastors of those churches, and at the voters league. I vowed never again to give aid or assistance to them, even though one of those pastors was or had been the president of the local Chapter of the NAACP, and an elected member of the City Council of Augusta, Georgia during that time.

March 20 was rapidly passing without any success in obtaining a place for King to speak on March 24. I decided not to call Reuben that afternoon or evening to inform him of my lack of success. I had to try again. I began to really understand what Joseph  must have experienced when he and Mary could not find a place where Christ could be born.

It was absolutely necessary to my soul, my innermost feeling that Dr. King revisit Augusta. My connection with him grew out of his visits to Howard University while I was in Howard University Law School. The unselfish demonstrations he had conducted, along with the rest of us, facing personal injury from racist police officers and their dogs, even death as he nonviolently marched throughout the South to break down barriers of segregation; the talk about him. The jeers and name calling by a one-time governor of Georgia who vowed that if King led a demonstration in Georgia in violation of Georgia Law, he would place him so deep in the common jail, he would have to have air pumped to him, to stay alive. An indelible picture of King appeared in my mind, and I could not let go of it. The goals and aspirations he had for black folk in America were the same goals and aspirations I had.

The seriousness of purpose he brought to the Civil Rights Movement had been eating at my soul since I was ten years old. And he, above all others, had given life and meaning to those feelings I had wrestled with all of my life. I failed to understand how some black leaders in Augusta, Chicago, Detroit and around the nation could feel uncomfortable around Dr. King.

Feeling so strongly, I knew I must keep pushing, using every resource at my command to bring him to Augusta, even though time was running out. Further, I did not want it known that Dr. King was unwelcome in Augusta. It just did not seem right. It was not right. His rejection was unjustified. But then, I thought about the stone which the builders had rejected becoming the head of the corner. I knew Dr. King fit that mold.

That night, March 20, I made personal contact with Lester Strowbridge, the business agent of Local 1137, Labor's International Union, and with Reverend Vernon, the pastor of Beulah Grove Baptist Church. I also spoke to several members of an organization called

CCWC (Citizens Concerned about the Welfare of the Community) to get the benefit of their thoughts and suggestions. Reverend Vernon offered his church for the occasion. He stated that it was small, seating only 500 to 600 people, but we could use it if we so desired.

I was elated. Even though we expected 3000 to 6000 people would attend if the word got out that King was coming, the opportunity to bring him back to Augusta was paramount.

Reverend Vernon was cautioned how it might affect him, but he said if his church gave him approval and that was all he needed. What fellow pastors thought about him in this endeavor did not matter, he opined. The fact that Dr. King wanted to come back to Augusta and would come back in seeking support for the Poor People's Campaign, and he and his church could be a part of this historic occasion, was enough to arouse excitement in him.

You could see it in the broad smile he displayed when things were right and God-like. Neither he, nor the rest of us, hesitated or equivocated about our mission. The question now was, how do we get the word out? And was 2:30 p.m. a convenient time for Dr. King to speak to a large crowd on that Saturday, March 24, 1968?

All we knew and needed to know at that time was that Dr. King was returning to Augusta and we would be a part of that event. It thrilled all of us.

The next day, March 21, 1968, a Wednesday, I telephoned Reuben Gamble and confirmed that I would sponsor King in Augusta. There were so many details to finalize. I wanted to know the time of his arrival so we could start our public announcement of his appearance. What mode of travel would he use? When were we to meet him? What kind of security was needed to protect him?  After all, Dr. King had so far escaped serious personal injury by the enforcement of strict security and adequate protection during demonstrations in other cities. He was about to go to Memphis to lead a march in support of that city's sanitation workers. A march where one person was killed and eight or more people  were injured.

The local public media and other anti-King characters used these incidents to further criticize Dr. King, and actually called him a man of violence even though they knew he was a disciple of nonviolence. These tactics were designed to minimize King's effectiveness, to frighten blacks away from King and make him look unpatriotic, disruptive and untrustworthy. Such measures had been used many years before during slavery days by the plantation owners and their overseers fostering dissension among blacks in any way possible. They had fomented fear, distrust and suspicion among the slaves to keep them from uniting to challenge the slave system.

When I made contact with Reuben, he told me that King's schedule had him in Albany, Georgia the morning of March 24, and he was not sure how long he would be there. He assured me he would let me know as soon as possible what time Dr. King would leave, how he would be traveling, what time he would get to Augusta, and where we could meet him. The scheduled visit was confirmed.

Final confirmation of his coming galvanized all of us into action regardless of what it might cost us socially, financially or politically.

For the first time I began to realize the awesome responsibility I had undertaken to bring Dr. King back to Augusta. Lester Strowbridge, my good friend, whose union office was in our building, and my secretary, Alberta Johnson and her husband John Henry Johnson, a mail carrier, along with my wife Charlotte, and Reverend B. I. Vernon were the only persons I confided in while planning this event.

Somewhere in this saga I forgot about my own personal safety and that of my children, who received telephone threats that I would be killed if I brought King back to Augusta. My complete concentration was on having a successful nonviolent gathering at Beulah Grove Baptist Church for the people to see and hear Dr. Martin Luther King, Jr., a world personality, and great world leader, one more time.

Little did I know at that time, of King's plans to go to Memphis to lead another march on April 5. I certainly never imagined that he would be assassinated before the march even began. So we all went about our tasks and assigned duties as we awaited word from Reuben Gamble.

In the meantime, I made contact with the only local black newspaper, *The Weekly Review*, and its publisher and editor, Reverend M. J. Whitaker, to see if that newspaper would run a news release of Dr. King's revisit to Augusta. Reverend Whitaker agreed to run the story if he received the information by 5:00 p.m. March 22, a Thursday.

Contact was also made with the daily *Augusta Chronicle* (morning paper), and *Augusta Herald* (evening paper) about running stories related to Dr. King's revisit to Augusta. I received no assurance that they would run the story or cover the event. It really did not concern me whether those newspapers made the announcements or not for we had the fastest news spreading vehicle in the world–telling each other by word of mouth.

Thursday morning Reuben Gamble called me at my office about 11:00 a.m., and informed me that Dr. King planned to leave Albany on Saturday, March 24 between 11:30 a.m. and 1:00 p.m. by private plane and would arrive in Augusta about 2:00 p.m. at Bush Field. The anticipation continued to build–I felt tense and anxious, but overjoyed.

The tension and anxiety increased by the hour. We had a day and a half to complete our preparations for King's visit. I called Bush Field, the local airport, to get instructions on how and where to assemble to meet the private plane transporting Dr. King. Would his plane be allowed to use the regular commercial plane landing runway? What gate would he enter? All of these details had to be finalized so our personal security team could be notified in time to plan adequately.

We had no idea who would be traveling with Dr. King and whether he would stay overnight. We hoped he would stay over so he could relax and discuss with the volunteers how to get involved in the Poor People's Campaign on Washington, and whether the wagon train was coming to Augusta. Excitement continued to build, rising to peak crescendo.

Reverend Vernon, of Beulah Grove was notified that Dr. King would be speaking, March 24. He was encouraged to prepare his church and congregation for Dr. King's arrival.

Reverend Vernon assured me that he and his church would be ready to meet Dr. King at any time during that Saturday. Now the pace had to be slowed down–anticlimactic feelings were creeping in. This spelled disaster, I thought.

Again I checked with the local newspapers asking for coverage of

Dr. King's visit, and I received a negative response. Knowing that we would have very little publicity about Dr. King's visit from the local media, news of this momentous occasion was delivered by word of mouth to as many people as we could talk to, and asked that they pass the word to others. Women of the Concerned Women's Club, the local SCLC Chapter, and Local 1137 used all the resources at their command to get the word out that Dr. King would be at Beulah Grove Baptist Church at 2:30 the coming Saturday, March 24, 1968.

Beulah Grove Baptist Church was located on Poplar Street. It was in a very poor neighborhood adjacent to a housing project and other single and double tenement houses. It was off and away from Gwinnett Street, the main thoroughfare in the black community, and its exact location was not widely known. It was small, but regardless of its size and location, I knew Dr. King would be welcomed and adequately protected, and that was all we desired. I felt as if I had not slept in days, nor had consumed a complete meal during those chaotic and pressured days.

It was decided that Lester Strowbridge would drive his car to Bush Field and act as the decoy car and I would drive my car and Dr. King would ride with me from the airport to the church. The route of travel would not be disclosed nor anyone informed of the type of transportation that would be used to transport Dr. King from the airport to the church. We would not disclose the exact arrival time of Dr. King's plane, nor the route to be taken to the church from Bush Field.

People started gathering at the church early Saturday morning and continued to arrive up to and after 2:30 p.m. The church filled to its capacity. Those who could not get into the church stood in the yard, all along Poplar and McCauley Streets.

The railroad tracks which ran in front of the church were covered with people. People from every nook and hamlet came to hear Dr. King, all except the black leadership in Augusta. They were nowhere to be found among the three or four thousand who had assembled. If they came they were incognito or as inconspicuous as possible. I am told that Jimmy Carter, himself an activist and supporter of our efforts in Augusta, and Reverend National Irvin were in attendance, but never made their presence known. Several white persons in Augusta voiced their intentions to attend, and did so with their children, especially Fay Hudson, a social worker and her children, and Leman Grier, an associate of Fay Hudson.

*Photo Credit: Melana Chaney*

*Bush Field Entrance*

*Photo Credit: Melana Chaney*

*The area where private planes arrive.*

*We waited anxiously for Dr. King's plane to arrive that day.*

# FOUR
## THE AIRPORT

*Let every voice sing, till earth and heaven ring;*

*Ring with the harmonies of liberty; Let our rejoicing rise,*

*high as the listening skies; Let it resound loud as the rolling sea.*

–Negro National Anthem

Early Saturday morning on March 24, I learned that Dr. King's plane would land in the area of Bush Field where private planes arrived and departed. I remembered distinctly a previous occasion on which I, as a member of a welcoming committee, met President Lyndon Johnson when he came to Augusta in 1964 during his campaign for President. I called and requested that Lester Strowbridge drive his car to that area at Bush Field and park his vehicle near where my vehicle would be parked, and to be there no later than 1:30 that afternoon

We arrived at Bush Field at 1:30 Saturday afternoon, March 24, 1968. The weather was clear and the sun was bright. We attempted to be inconspicuous as possible. We feared that someone there would recognize us and ask what was our purpose in being at Bush Field that day. We had not rehearsed what we would say if asked that question. Luckily for us, no one approached us—probably because we entered and exited the terminal in a most rapid manner on our way to the location where Dr. King's plane was to park for unloading.

The atmosphere was chilling. We were anxious and nervous. The thought of some people in high positions not wanting Dr. King to come to Augusta created a greater determination in us to carry out our mission. We tried to be as upbeat as possible. One cannot possibly describe the highs and lows we were experiencing. It seemed as if time stood still. We could hardly look each other in the face as we reached the unloading area.

Standing there waiting for Dr. King's plane to appear in the sky, we began to talk about the Poor People's Campaign. Since I was acquainted with Dr. King and Strowbridge was not, we decided that I would discuss that matter with him as well as any other issue we thought we should bring to his attention.

Augusta was simmering with discontent—a kind of quiet discord within the black community. Progress in school desegregation was very slow. The same old under-represented government continued insensitive to the needs of the black community. One could still hear police motorcycle riders blasting words such as "nigger" and "darky" from its speakers. Black men and women were still being "roughed-up" by local police and only one black was on the city police force. None were in the Richmond County Sheriff's Department, which was then under Sheriff J. T. Plunkett.

Droves of black women still congregated on work days at H. L. Green's drug store in the early morning hours at 9th Street (now James Brown Boulevard) and Broad Street to catch the city buses to take them to the hill to work for white people. They cleaned their homes, washed their clothes, cooked their meals, and baby-sat their children. For the most part, these women's own children were left at home unfed, unbathed, and unattended. It reverberated in our minds that things would not change… the more they seemed to change, the more they remained the same. This situation was totally unacceptable to us. The city of Augusta was polarized. White people knew why and none came forward to help bring the people together.

The hours passed. It was now 4:30 p.m. and King's plane was nowhere in sight.

Uneasiness and doubt gripped us. Would Dr. King come? What was happening? We began to wonder if the crowd, some 3,000 to 4,000 persons we had been told, was still waiting for us to bring Dr. King to Beulah Grove Baptist Church. Would they continue to wait? and for how long?

Thoughts of King's failure to come to Augusta engulfed me. Those who daringly, and without the blessing of the black leadership, had arranged this visit would be blamed. This would give those who disliked me, or were jealous of my influence in the Augusta area, an opportunity to rein in this so-called "stray horse," this "runaway mustang." Such a situation would lift their spirits knowing the failure of the one person in Augusta who had "peeped" their "hole card," and who knew they were out for personal gain rather than to improve the quality of life for all Augustans and particularly black Augustans. But this was not to be, at least not that day.

At approximately 4:45 that afternoon we received word from airport authorities that King had been delayed in Albany and that his plane would arrived at 5:30 p.m. This was joyful news. It brightened our hearts. What had been a somber and listless afternoon at a small airport in Augusta, Georgia, was being replaced with an afternoon of great anticipation. Strowbridge and I breathed sighs of relief and looked at each other in amazement. We realized that God had taken control of the events that were unfolding and we were just the instruments through which He was working. We had been snatched from defeat and disappointment to victory and jubilation. We almost cried in joy together.

As we watched the sky at about 5:20 p.m. the news came that King's plane would be landing in about ten minutes. Shortly thereafter the small two engine plane carrying Dr. King appeared, dropping from the sky. We could hardly contain ourselves. Of course, the thought of all those people having to wait so long for his appearance was ever present. Would they have waited three and a half hours to see and hear one man?

But this was not just one man. This was all of us wrapped up into one individual. This was the world-renowned Dr. Martin Luther King, Jr. Certainly they would wait.

The plane landed and taxied to the area where we were waiting. The engines shut down and the plane's passenger door unlocked and opened. First, to our pleasant surprise, Reverend Ralph Abernathy came out of the plane was greeted by me and Mr. Strowbridge. Then Dr. King came out with his sons, Dexter and Martin. It was a sight to behold!

As he walked down the steps I remembered how he looked the last time I had seen him at Tabernacle Baptist Church in Augusta some four or five years before, and how he had appeared as a much younger man at Howard University in the late fifties. The changes in him were obvious. The stress associated with his mission had taken its toll.

Here before us was the heart, the soul, the nerve, the reality and the true meaning of the Civil Rights movement. Here was the man who, more than any other man, had taken the fight of the oppressed to their oppressors in this so called "land of the free and home of the brave."

Dr. King was hatless and dressed in a silk green single-breasted suit. Elegantly attired and mannered, he looked a sure and determined business man, attentive to his surroundings and familiarizing himself in a polite way with all of us there. This proud looking man looked nothing like the man on television about whom a lot of bad things had been said. He looked, walked, dressed and talked like us. He actually was one of us… on a mission to improve the quality of life for millions of Americans. He exuded a restrained, controlled power.

"Dr. King," I said in a voice that was as "black clergy" as one could get, humble and lowly but not servile.

"I remember you. How are you?" he asked. His handshake was tight and quick.

It was mesmerizing.

"I am fine, now," I said.

"Oh, you didn't think we were going to make it," he laughed. But the laughter was one of extreme seriousness. He was obviously subdued.

"We sure didn't," I said, attempting to respond in like manner.

"I am terribly sorry we are so late, but matters beyond our control kept us in Albany longer than we expected. I will tell you about them later, but I think we had better get on to the church or wherever you have planned for us to be," he stated as he glanced around looking for his pilot.

"Here I am, Dr. King," the pilot said, emerging from underneath the plane.

"I just want you to know," Dr. King said to his pilot, "we will be here for some time and, of course, for dinner," Dr. King said, turning to get my reaction.

"Then I will stay around the terminal here and await further instructions," the pilot said.

"Thanks, we will be in touch," he informed the pilot.

It appeared that there were plans to stay overnight but he did not disclose his specific plans to me and I did not ask. Perhaps he would tell me later, I thought.

After retrieving what looked like an overnight bag, all of us, King, Dexter, Martin, Strowbridge and I started walking to our cars parked near by out of the public's view. We did not have to go back through the terminal.

It was getting dark. Abernathy and King's son, Martin, III, got in the car with Strowbridge and King and his son, Dexter, got into my Chrysler Imperial. Strowbridge, following our prearranged plans, left the airport on the main road to Augusta and entered Olive Road, the back way, to get to Beulah Grove. I was to go out Tobacco Road, and drive into Augusta by way of Savannah Road. We felt pretty safe with these arrangements.

Dr. King got in the passenger side of my car and Dexter sat on the back seat behind his father. I drove slowly out of Bush field hoping we would not draw attention from those coming into the airport.

"Well, how are my friends here in Augusta–you know, the ones who were at Morehouse with me and were instrumental in arranging our first visit to Augusta?" asked Dr. King.

"I suppose they are doing well–I have not seen or had contact with them in several days," I said. The friends he was referring to were those persons whom we had asked to assist us in bringing him to Augusta, the ones who had frowned upon his visit, but I did not tell him that. I wanted his short stay to be pleasant and enjoyable.

"Tell me," I asked, "Just how is the Poor People's March on Washington coming?"

King turned and looked at me and smiled, his lips tightened.

"What do they call you by name?  I am talking about your associates?" he asked.

"They call me John," I said. "I was called Johnny when I was at

Howard Law School," I continued.

"So you went to Howard. I had a classmate at Morehouse who went to Howard Law School. You know him–his name is Bennie Harris."

"Sure, I know Bennie. He was my best friend at Howard," I said. Everyone knew Bennie. He was smart, witty, and talkative. Bennie always wanted to be like Howard Thurmond from Boston University School of Theology, Mordecai Johnson, President of Howard, and most of all Dr. Benjamin Mays, President of Morehouse. His walk and talk telegraphed these aspirations to those who knew him.

*Beulah Grove Baptist Church*

*Reverend Vernon began the service with prayer.*

# FIVE
## THE MEETING
## AT THE CHURCH

*I have been to the mountain top;*

*I've seen the Promised Land. I may not get there with you,*

*but one day we as a people will get to the Promised Land.*

*–Dr. Martin Luther King, Jr.*

**"W**hy don't you let me call you 'Wat' and you call me 'Martin,'" Dr. King asked.

"That's okay with me–sounds good," I said.

"We thought we were going to have to give up our Poor People's March on Washington. We did not have enough money to pay for the things we needed to take care of the people while in Washington, to accommodate all the people while in Washington, all the people we expect to attend. It will be like the one in 1963," he stated.

"But, you know, Wat," he continued. "I got a call just before we landed from Henry Ford. He said that the Ford Foundation will donate $250,000.00 to the Poor People's March. That promise has given us additional strength to forge on. And now I believe we will make it," he said.

The conversation continued and we developed a respectful rapport. By that time we were coming down McCauley Street from deep inside of Sunset Homes Housing Project, about two blocks from the church.

As we approached the church, King leaned forward to see the faces of the hundreds of people who had come to see him. He made every effort to smile. I sensed a little nervousness about him which I had not noticed before. Things got quiet as we pulled up in front of the church from on Poplar Street. Very few persons there at the church knew King was riding with me. But as soon as he exited the car, throngs gathered to see him. He waved and walked briskly into the church.

Abernathy was already inside the church. A television crew from NBC news had set up the necessary equipment to tape the event. Herb Kapflo from NBC news was visible throughout. He had a seat in the choir box where he could see and record every word and move that King made. This made me uneasy. I was concerned that he would be so close to us.

It was dark and getting late. All the people in the church stood to welcome Dr. King as he walked down the aisle to the pulpit.

Who would believe that ten days later this fine and deeply religious man would be killed? It is well that we had no way of knowing about the coming tragic event.

Reverend Vernon, after the crowd became quiet, strode to the lectern, glanced over the audience and said:

"We are so grateful to have you all here and we apologize for the long wait, but you see," he said, as he looked around at Dr. King, "the wait was worth it." Thunderous applause erupted.

In the pulpit, Dr. King sat to my left in the minister's chair and to my right sat Dr. Abernathy. Other ministers whom I had never seen before nor since that night also were sitting on the platform.

"This is a momentous occasion for Beulah Grove and the people of Augusta," Reverend Vernon said. "I am overwhelmed and delighted to be here with you," he continued.

King's sons sat just in front and to the right of the pulpit in front of the NBC news crew. They looked and listened in a disciplined manner.

There were no printed programs showing the order of service. Reverend Vernon was a master at ad-libbing in these kind of instances. His performance was so dignified. He was an outstanding gentlemen under pressure even though he was extremely nervous. In fact we all were nervous and anxious. Dr. King seemed to be settling down. He forced a smile as he slumped down in the huge minister's chair.

"Now I want all of you to give a resounding applause for Reverend Ralph Abernathy, who will in turn introduce our speaker for this occasion," Reverend Vernon concluded, as the crowd began to applaud.

Abernathy, a short stocky person, very well dressed for this event, rose to take the podium to introduce Dr. King.

The audience became very, very quiet; almost eerily quiet. They had come to hear Dr. King. They wanted Abernathy to say a few words

*Reverend Abernathy introduced Dr. King.*

*Dr. King at the lectern, beginning his short, but eloquent, speech.*

and then sit down. But Abernathy wanted to make a speech and he began:

"We have come a long ways, and we ain't goin' to let nobody turn us back now," he stated in a deep monologue voice.

"You know our struggles have paid off in several ways but we are still poor and most of us are uneducated. That is why we come to you this evening," he said.

"See, you know we have come a long way because I now have a white secretary working in our offices–who would have dreamed that I would have a white secretary?" he asked.

The audience was not interested in this kind of rhetoric and neither was I so I leaned over and whispered to Dr. King, "Can you stop him from going on like this–we are not interested in who is or is not working in his office," I said.

"That's Ralph for you, Wat," King said to me. "Let him talk on. You cannot stop him once he gets going," he said.

Finally Reverend Abernathy started talking about Dr. King.

"I am delighted to be a partner of the man I call my true friend. I will not go into who he is or what he stands for," he exclaimed. "You know him–he is known the world over. We have been mostly everywhere together–in jail together, marching together, praying together–always struggling together! And we will continue until all the walls of segregation and inequality in America fall down," he said.

"So it always gives me great pleasure to introduce and present my great friend and partner, Martin Luther King," he announced.

The audience jumped to its feet with thunderous applause as Dr. King looked at me and got up from the oak arm chair and stepped to the podium. He took a sip from a glass of water that was sitting on the right side of the podium as the applause and cheers continued.

His eyes seem to have gotten larger and his stance at the podium was nothing less than magnificent. He stood there for a few minutes holding onto the podium with both hands as he leaned backwards; he was in control. He did not have any notes or a written speech and as the audience quieted and sat down, he said:

"I want to apologize for being so late. But you know sometimes if you just wait good things will come to you." he said in reference to the call he had received from Henry Ford, but he did not explain.

For some reason he never did look at the NBC cameraman or its reporter. He looked from his right to his left and began speaking in a quiet, deliberate fashion that was not his normal style. The audience was quiet but anxious, and ready for Dr. King to make them feel good. They knew the kind of speeches he could make and they were ready. They knew he was explosive and they were ready for him to explode.

"Reverend Vernon and Brother Watkins, I want to thank you and all those who assisted in our visit again to Augusta," he said as he turned to look back at Reverend Vernon and myself and the other pulpit guests.

"I know you have made a tremendous sacrifice in arranging this affair, and I want to thank you for all that you have done in bringing us here on our last stop, in our drive to finance the Poor People's Campaign on Washington to be held later next month."

You and those who have assisted you will never be forgotten," he said, his voice rising. "We know and appreciate how you have worked to make this a successful affair."

"There are those who would like for us to fail in this endeavor. But I tell you they will not succeed in their efforts, for we are doing God's will," he thundered and the audience went wild, standing and cheering him on. He waited for the applause to stop and then he said:

"This country has lost its sense of direction, its sense of purpose and it needs to rearrange it priorities. For we cannot fight an immoral war in Vietnam where many of our young men are dying and at the same time finance the war on poverty to help our people in this country–white and black people living in what seem like hopeless conditions. And I would be remiss if I did not try to do something about it," he shouted.

"Let them think of me as they like. As long as breath is in this body, I am going to do whatever I can to eliminate these conditions so when our boys come home, we can truly help the poor and uneducated. This is what the Poor People's March is all about, and we ask for your support in this noble crusade. Can I count on you to help me?" he asked.

The audience stood to applaud him as he returned to the big oak chair. His speech was short and most of us were disappointed it did not last longer, but we felt good.

Dr. King told me as he returned and sat down that he was tired and hungry and that they had arranged to eat dinner at the Uptowner Motel as soon as the meeting was over. I got the point and assured him that I would drive him and his sons there immediately. He did not wish to remain after the meeting, but said he wanted to talk to me about a few things over dinner. I really felt relieved and happy about the success of our gathering, but I could not but wonder what it was that he wanted to discuss with me. I would soon find out.

*Photo Credit: Kathy Davis Watkins*

*Photo Credit: Kathy Davis Watkins*

*The Lorraine Motel. The room where Dr. King was to sleep the night of April 4, 1968.*

# SIX
# DINNER AND ONE-ON-ONE CONVERSATION WITH KING

*If a man does not have anything worth dying for*

*he is not fit to live.*

–Dr. Martin Luther King, Jr.

We arrived at the Uptowner Motel at about 9:30 p.m. that evening. When he exited my car, Dr. King asked that I get his bags from the trunk. I thought then he was planning to stay overnight. I told him how glad I was that he was relaxing and what a good night's sleep would do for him.

He looked so tired and kind of desperate. He seemed burdened with some inexplicable problems. Something very deep was disturbing him, and it began to show in his face.

We walked into the motel and were immediately directed to the dining room. It was empty. I wondered why and then I began to admit to myself that I was, and had been afraid for all of us. I had noticed several white men standing around in the lobby of the motel looking strange. I later discovered that these men were tracking King and myself.

Funny, I never saw Abernathy at the motel. Strowbridge told me the following Monday that he had dropped Abernathy and his son off at the motel before King, Dexter and I had arrived.

A waiter approached our table to take the orders. I cannot remember what King or his sons ordered. I had a cup of coffee, my appetite had not returned. It appeared that they had pre-registered for King was in no hurry to finish his meal and his sons slumbered or walked about the motel but were not out of sight of us as we talked.

"Wat," King began, "our big problems in America are economics and education. Too few people own most of the wealth and they are not about to share it with us.

Unless we find a way to break this economic stronghold on us and are allowed to share in the vast wealth of this country, we will always be on the bottom.

There are those who criticize me because of my stand against the Vietnam War; some of my colleagues have personally attacked me, and have shunned me because of that, but I don't care," he said. "It is a waste of lives and money. Money that could be used here in America. Some bad things are being told about me by the little man in Washington. But I am not afraid of him or anyone else. I shall continue to speak out against this evil war."

"I wouldn't pay that any attention," I said. "You are a great man and we all love and respect you," I said, knowing that the persons he was talking about were just jealous and desperate, and really afraid of him and his power.

"You know I must go to Memphis to show all who think otherwise that I can and will lead a peaceful march," he said.

"But first I must go to Chicago to check on Jesse. We need to talk seriously with him and get a clear understanding of why some things that are hurting our cause," he said. He never informed me what those "things" were and I never asked. In later years I learned what those "things" were, and I, too, was disappointed.

"Do you think you should go back to Memphis?" I asked. "After all, there seems to be a lot of violence brewing there. It could be dangerous," I said.

"Yes, you may be right. But I must show everyone that I can still lead a nonviolent march. I must go there also for the sanitation workers," he said. "We will finish what we started."

"Is it absolutely necessary that you go to Memphis?" I asked.

"Afraid so. Why don't you join us or at least join the Poor People's March?" he asked.

"I wish I could but my children need me here with them and I cannot leave," I said. "But let me know what else I can do."

"Wat, I don't know what we will do if the Poor People's Campaign does not bring about direct attention and change for the betterment of our people.

I have some other ideas about which I have not talked to anyone but since we are getting that money from Ford Foundation, one of those ideas, if implemented, may hurt the very people who are genuinely with us in this crusade if we put those plans into operation," he stated.

I remained noncommittal. I had no idea what he was talking about. Now his facial expression was one of anxiety and I knew he was dead serious.

"This country really does not care about its poor, particularly the black poor. Oh, they will talk about it when it is convenient for their purposes. But by and large the American Congress isn't really committed to helping the poor and, in particular, black poor people," he said.

"I thought President Johnson's War on Poverty was directed to helping the poor, including black people," I stated.

"He is headed in the right direction but I do not believe his heart is in it," he stated. "The attention he has to give to the war in Vietnam and the financing of it; and the demonstrations against that war by college students occupy his mind most of the time. It is going to take a shocking event here at home to get him to focus his attention on America's problems… on poor people's problems here at home."

"Like what?" I asked.

"Well," he said, "The big corporations and those who run them are getting richer and richer off of the war, and too many of our young men are dying in such an immoral conflict," he continued.

I, too, knew that the children and relatives of the rich and famous were not going to Vietnam.

"If we can stop the war, some of that money could be used to address the many problems of the poor and most of all save the lives of thousands of black America boys. That is what I want to see happen. Do you agree?" he asked.

"Sure," I said. "But suppose the war is brought to an end and your hopes and dreams, as well as mine, do not materialize because Washington will not support your efforts," I continued.

This is getting pretty deep for me, I thought. He was now talking like a person who had become frustrated in his efforts to reach the goals he had set for himself. Almost like a defeatist attitude.

It reminded me of Goldwater in the "extremism" speech he made when he spoke at the Republican National Convention in 1964.

What was King willing to do to keep his dreams alive? Further, why was he sharing these things with me? What was now motivating this wonderful person who had gained so much prominence and had done so much good for so many of my people? Was the $250,000.00 grant from the Ford Foundation fodder for this changed attitude from the one he had so eloquently displayed in his "I Have A Dream" speech in Washington in 1963? Or was it something deep in his soul just now surfacing? I asked myself.

Then he began to bare his heart. He shared about all he had been through. He still felt he had not done enough to help the poor to become educated, to make money, to acquire wealth to help themselves. We discussed what were perhaps the most important items needed to eliminate the problems of the poor… money and education. We concurred that it does not always take education to make money, but it always takes education to maintain and wisely use money once it is acquired.

He felt that a new tactic should be employed to try to solve an ancient problem… the problem that no one is going to give the poor his hard earned money or a portion of his inheritance without something beneficial to him or her in return. The crux of the problem was how to extract money from the richest Americans to be used to educate the poorest Americans, so they could survive and co-exist in the world's richest country, and pursue the same dream that every other American had reached for and achieved.

King leaned over and almost in a whisper told me what he planned to do.

Then he continued, "This will work. If those who have supported us in the past will support us in this effort. It is drastic, and I firmly believed that only drastic actions bring forth drastic change."

It scared me nearly to death as I thought about it. Had this man gone crazy–had he lost his mind? Didn't he know that if the kind of program he was contemplating were put into action and were supported as he thinks it would be supported, like the Montgomery Bus Boycott, the devastating effect it would bring upon the people of this country, and especially the rich? This would even hurt directly the man whose foundation had just donated $250,000.00 to his Poor People's March on Washington. He said he knew that but he hoped that it would not come to that.

I promised him that I would not mention his idea to anyone. I expressed my hope it would never be activated, and that we could go on waging the fight for poor people in ways such as the Poor People's March on Washington.

I had heard enough. I wondered if anyone had overheard our conversation. I had this strange feeling like someone was behind us. It was getting late.

"I love my people and there is nothing legitimate I would not do to see that our people are free from the terrible ways in which so many have to live," he said.

"I must go now, Martin," I said. "It is getting late and you need all the rest you can get before going to Chicago."

"You're right, Wat," he said. His sons had rejoined us and were struggling to keep awake. They were such handsome children, I thought as I studied them, wondering if they would be like their dad. I also wondered about my own children following in my footsteps.

I got up from the table to leave and Martin got up, but I said, "Please, you do not have to come to the lobby with me."

"I know," he said as he grasped my hand and patted me on the back. He had loosened his tie and seemed more relaxed.

"I do hope you join the march–I do not know if it will come through Augusta," he said.

"If it does, I'll be there. Tell Hosea I said hello." I said. Hosea Williams was a member of King's inner circle, a man I had first  met in Savannah while I was a student of Savannah State College as it was called at that time.

"I'll be glad to," he said.

As I walked through the dining room to the lobby of the motel, I turned to look back and he was watching me. I exited the motel still in a mild state of shock and wondering what would happen next in this great man's life. I was soon to find out.

*Mr. John D. Watkins on Beale Street in Memphis, TN.*

*Martin Luther King, Jr. Memorial.*

# SEVEN
## KING'S DEATH
## AND AFTERMATH

*Precious Lord, take my hand; lead me on; let me stand.*

*I am tired; I am weak; I am worn; thru the storm, thru the night.*

*Lead me on to the light. Take my hand, precious Lord, lead me home…*

*and when the day is past and gone, at the river I stand,*

*Guide my feet, hold my hand.  Take my hand, precious Lord, lead me home.*

To add insult to one of the greatest injuries done to mankind, a memorial service was conducted in Augusta one day after King's assassination. It was held in one of the churches which denied him access during his last visit to the city only ten days before.

None of us who had brought King to Augusta were invited. It was, to say the least, a disgusting sight. In attendance and in the pulpit of that church were the very people who had, on March 24, refused to greet King or attend the church where he was speaking: a white state Senator, Augusta's white Mayor, the white President of the Chamber of Commerce, and the black minister of that church who happened to be a member of the Augusta City Council. This array of those who opposed King, in that church, on that day, served its purpose–to quiet the voices which could stir violence in the city–as was happening all over America.

The calm only endured for two years. On May 11, 1970 a riot broke out in Augusta. Burning, looting, and murder occurred in scores of stores burned, but only in the black community. Race relations were set back for at least 50 years or perhaps longer.

But the stone which the builders had rejected indeed became the head of the corner.

Martin Luther King, Jr.'s visit to Augusta on that Saturday in March, ten days before his tragic death in Memphis, lives on in our memory, and his presence among us is illuminated on every anniversary of that visit.

I went to Atlanta for his funeral. I wanted to pay my last personal respects to him. We walked in the middle of Hunter Street in Atlanta, far behind the wagon carrying his body. Thousands of people were there to show their respect to this great man.

I took my two oldest children, David and Crystal, to this momentous and historical event so they could get the feel of and appreciate this great man. Maybe some day they would explain to their children what had been happening in America while he led the struggle to make men and women free. To understand that he gave his life for our freedom, and to the world as an example of how to fight oppression without war.

We never got very close to the coffin, but we were close enough to see the casket being taken from the wagon. It made me think about President Kennedy's funeral and I wondered how his wife, Coretta, and the other children were holding up in this very sad and painful time.

We then returned to Augusta, still in shock and unable to discuss what we had witnessed.

I asked myself over and over again, as I ask myself to this day, "Who and why did they have to kill him?' Perhaps someday we will know.

Ten days to the hour that Dr. King was in Augusta, April 4, 1968, an assassin fired the fatal shot that ended his life. I was in a state of paralysis for days. It was like my own life had been taken away. I had known that evening, but why I knew I didn't know, that if he returned to Memphis to help his friends something was going to happen to him, and look what happened, I thought.

"Greater love hath no man than he who lays down his life for his friends." This is what makes clear the old utterance that "The dependence of a great man upon a greater man is a subjection that lower men cannot easily understand."

# EPILOGUE



*The Lord is my Shepherd, I shall not want. He maketh me to lie down in*

*green pastures; He leadeth me beside the still waters; He restoreth my soul.*

*He leadeth me in the path of righteousness for His name's sake.*

*Yea, though I walk through the valley of the shadow of death, I will fear*

*no evil; for Thou art with me; Thy rod and Thy staff they comfort me.*

*Thou preparest a table before me in the presence of mine enemies;*

*Thou anointest my head with oil; My cup runneth over.*

*Surely goodness and mercy shall follow me all the days of my life;*

*And I shall dwell in the house of the Lord forever.*

*–Psalm 23*

That King would be the victim of a bullet fired from the rifle of a white assassin begs the question… How could such a thing happen? That this assassin would be one James Earl Ray, a low, low, lowly white thug and bank robber is beyond belief. It is so shocking that such a great man would be brought down by a drifter–an incongruity that will require the history of assassins and their personalities to be reexamined. How can the human mind really imagine one cut-rate robbing white thug committing such a terrible act alone? Americans, black and white, find it hard to believe, and most reject the theory that Ray acted alone.

Well, this conniving bank robber, con artist did act alone in firing the rifle which killed Dr. King on April 4, 1968 as he stood on the balcony of the Lorraine Motel in Memphis, Tennessee. But in the overall scheme of things, many, many others were involved. It may never be known who the others were unless one of those involved, or one of his descendants, so troubled by his conscience that he cannot rest, steps forth to disclose the identity of the others involved.

But the questions which trouble us the most are: How did Ray know: (1) that King would be staying at the Lorraine Motel on April 4, 1968? (2) what room he would be occupying? (3) and that he would be standing on the balcony just outside that room at the particular time when the one fatal shot would be fired? Who gave this information to James Earl Ray and Why? We can only inescapably conclude that there had to have been others involved who gave this detailed information to Ray to enable him to position himself to fire the shot that was heard around the world.

Dr. King's death in such a manner by such a person acting without the assistance of others, was, and always will be, totally unacceptable; it defies history.

The violent deaths of black revolutionaries in America, known and unknown, whatever their goals may have been, at the hands of white men, have been effected by the concerted efforts of more than one white man through lynchings, burnings, beatings, kidnappings and state executions, and usually done in the early evening or the middle of the night. The same insidious efforts surround the assassination of perhaps America's greatest gift to mankind.

These are the traits of cold blooded killers.

Dr. King's violent death left black Americans numb and leaderless; like a ship without a rudder or a flying airplane whose pilot has been stricken by heart failure. Where they go and take those aboard no one knows. We do know that ships will cease to sail and planes will cease to fly and generally those aboard and their philosophies of doing things will be scattered throughout the world for others to imitate. But one thing is for sure… those who participate in such ennoble events make sure there will be a cessation of that revolutionary's efforts, if only temporarily. If perchance others take up the mission, the culprits know it will be without the great impetus and fervor of the deceased revolutionary. His goal is then less likely to be achieved, if at all, ever achieved, but their followers do remember:

*Great men all remind us we can make our lives sublime and departing leave behind us footprints on the sands of time.*

# WORDS OF INSPIRATION

The following are words of inspiration to King and those who still believe in a true America.

*My country, tis of thee, Sweet land of liberty,*
*Of thee, I sing; Land where our fathers died,*
*Land of the Pilgrim's pride; From every mountain side,*
*Let Freedom ring.*

We hold these truths to be self-evident that all men are created equal. That they are endowed by their Creator with certain unalienable rights, amongst these are: Life, Liberty and the Pursuit of Happiness.

*Declaration of Independence*

Fourscore and seven years ago, Our Fathers brought forth upon this continent a new nation, conceived in Liberty and dedicated to the proposition that all men are created equal.

*Lincoln's Gettysburg Address*

Men should not be judged by the color of their skin, but by the content of their character.

*Martin Luther King, Jr.*

If a man does not have anything worth dying for he is not fit to live.

*Martin Luther King, Jr.*

The only thing we have to fear is fear itself.

*Franklin D. Roosevelt*

I have been to the mountain top…I have seen the Promised Land. I may not get there with you, but one way we as a people will get to the Promised Land.

*Martin Luther King, Jr.*

Ask not what your country can do for you, but ask what you can do for your country.

*John F. Kennedy*

Men see things and ask why… I dream things that never were, and ask why not.

*Robert L. Kennedy*

Let every voice sing, till earth and heaven ring,
Ring with the harmonies of liberty;
Let our rejoicing rise, high as the listening skies,
Let it resound loud as the rolling sea.

*Negro National Anthem*

The Lord is my Shepherd, I shall not want. He maketh me to lie down in green pastures; He leadeth me beside still waters; he restoreth my sou. He leadeth me in the path of righteousness for his name's sake. Yea, tho I walk through the valley of the shadow of death, I will fear no evil; for Thou art with me; Thy rod and Thy staff they comfort me. Thou preparest a table before me in the presence of mine enemies; Thou anointest my head with oil; my cup runneth over. Surely goodness and mercy shall follow me all the days of my life; And I will dwell in the house of the Lord forever.

*Psalm 23*

Precious Lord, take my hand, Lead me on, let me stand. I am  weak, I
am worn; Thru the storm, thru the night, Lead me on to the light,
Take my hand, precious Lord, Lead me home.
When my way grows drear, precious Lord, linger near.
When my life is almost gone, hear my cry,
Hold my hand lest I fall;
Take my hand, precious Lord, lead me home.
When the darkness appears and the night draws near,
And the day is past and gone,
At the river I stand, Guide my feet, hold my hand;
Take my hand, precious Lord, Lead me home.

We Shall Overcome One Day

*The Civil Rights Song*


Oh, beautiful for spacious skies, for amber waves of grain,
For purple mountains majesties, Above the fruited plain!
America! America! God shed his grace on thee,
And crown thy good with brotherhood
From sea to shining sea.

*America the Beautiful*


It would be sure folly to entrust the enforcement or protection of the
Civil Rights of Americans of color to black men and women whose
salaries are paid by a state or local government when the constituents
of that government are white and in the majority.


He has urged cruel war against human nature, violating its most sacred
rights of life and liberty in the persons of a distant people who never
offended him, capturing and carrying them into slavery in another
hemisphere or to incur miserable death in their transportation.
*These words were omitted from the Declaration of Independence*

"The scenes of this story, as its title indicates, lie among a race heretofore ignored by the association of polite and refined society: An exotic race whose ancestors, born beneath a tropic sun, brought with them, and perpetuated to their descendants, a character so essentially unlike the hard and dominant Anglo-Saxon race, as for many years to have won from it only misunderstanding and contempt.

In this general movement, unhappy Africa at last is remembered; Africa, who began the race of civilization and human progress in the dim, gray dawn of early times, but who, for centuries, has lain bound and bleeding at the foot of civilized and Christianized humanity, imploring compassion in vain."

*Harriet Beecher Stowe, Uncle Tom's Cabin*

# BIBLIOGRAPHY

1.  The Augusta Chronicle

2.  DAVIS, BURKE
    Sherman's March, New York, 1980

3.  DAVIS, KENNETH
    Don't Know Much about the Civil War, New York, 1996

4.  FREEDMAN, RUSSELL
    Lincoln, a Photo-Biography, New York, 1987

5.  GADSTONE, WILLIAM A.
    United States Colored Troops, Gettysburg, 1990

6.  GARRISON, WEBB
    A Treasury of Civil War Tales, Nashville, TN, 1988

7.  LENZ, RICHARD J.
    The Civil War in Georgia, Watkinsville, GA, 1995

8.  McPHERSON, JAMES M.
    The Civil War, New York, NY

9.  McPHERSON, JAMES AND MONT. KURSTER,
    Images of the Civil War, New York, NY, 1992

10. MYRDAL, GUNNER
    An American Dilemma, Volume II, The Negro Problem
    and Modern Democracy, New Brunswick, NJ, 1996

11.  ROSENFIELD, RICHARD N.
American Aurora, New York, NY, 1997

12.  STERLING, DOROTHY
The Trouble They Seen, New York, NY, 1976

13.  STOWE, HARRIETT BEECHER
Uncle Tom's Cabin, New York, NY, 1967)

14.  THOMAS, VELMA MAIG
Lest We Forget, New York, NY, 1997

15.  WATCH TOWER BIBLE AND TRACT SOCIETY
of Pennsylvania, Brooklyn, NY, 1961, and 1981